CW01654196

The Great Western System

This map gives a general indication of where the locomotives in this book were to be found at work. It illustrates the extent of the Great Western Railway at its zenith in the 1930s. Limitations of space prevent more detailed coverage, particularly in the London, Bristol, West Midlands and South Wales areas.

The author of this Series is the founder of the Bressingham Steam Museum, with a large range of engines, road, rail and stationary. Several locomotives are in steam for rides, etc. on open days, mainly Sunday and Thursday afternoons May to September. Bressingham is near Diss, midway between Norwich and Ipswich.

The compiler of this Series is the Chairman, Magazine Editor and a steam loco driver of the Severn Valley Railway Company, which operates a 12-mile-long line between Bridgnorth, Shropshire and Bewdley, Worcestershire. Over thirty steam locos are based on the system and frequent services are run from March to October in the superb setting of the Severn Valley.

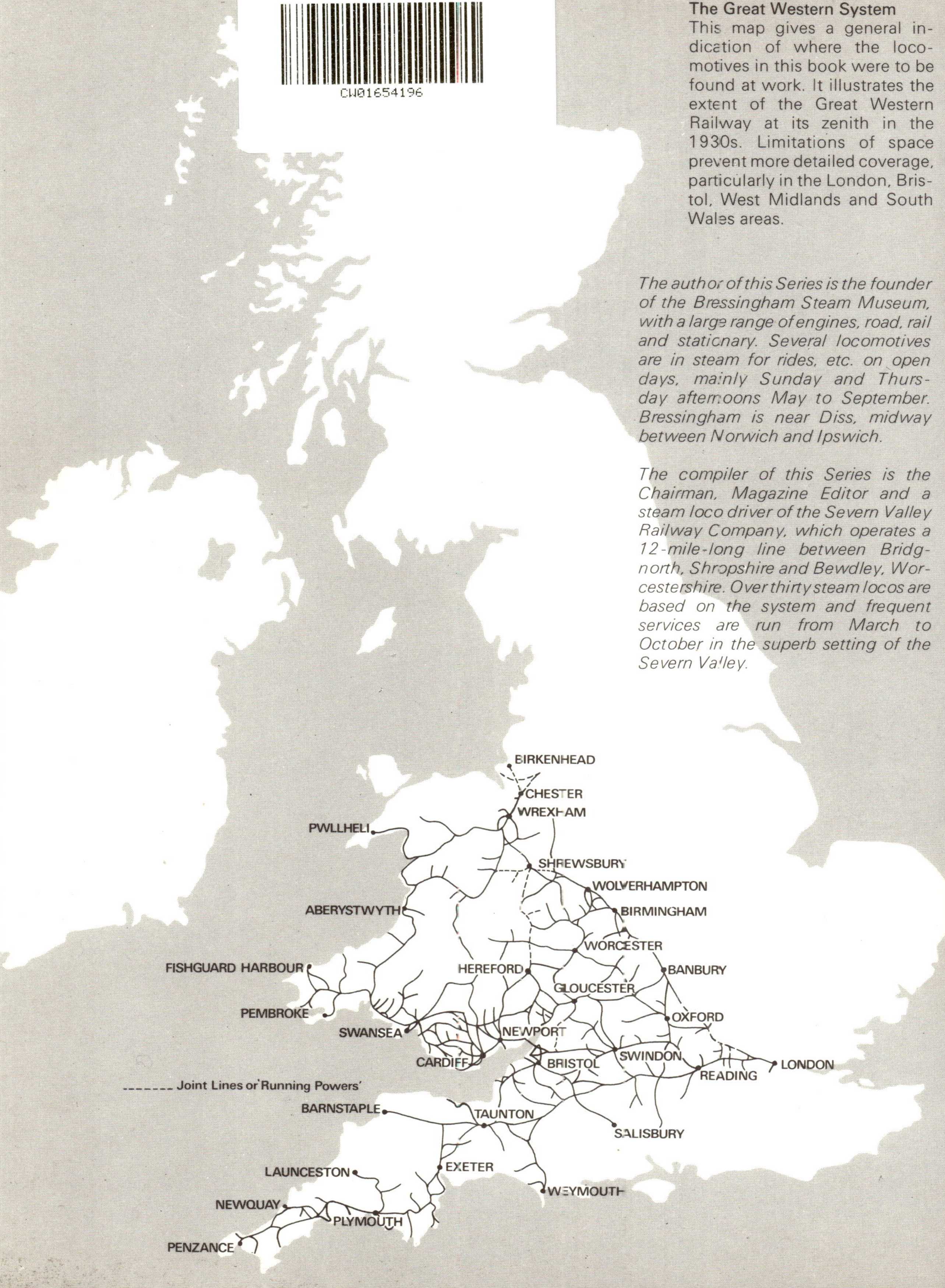

Jarrold Railway Series 1

Locomotives of the Great Western Railway

Written by Alan Bloom *Compiled by David Williams*

Locomotives of the Great Western Railway

Written by Alan Bloom
Compiled by David Williams

Front Cover: To celebrate the fiftieth birthday of the pioneer 'King' 4–6–0, a trip was run from Newport, Gwent, to Shrewsbury and back. Here No. 6000 *King George V* heads the Severn Valley Railway's train of Great Western restored coaches northwards at Caerleon on 3 July 1977. The 4–6–0, part of the National Collection, was restored to service by Bulmers Cider. (*D. C. Williams*)

Back Cover: 0–6–0 pannier tank No. 5764 crosses Victoria Bridge across the River Severn on the frosty morning of 4 December 1976. It is heading a train of Great Western coaches between Bewdley and Arley on the Severn Valley Railway. (*D. C. Williams*)

When the four great Railway companies were submerged under Nationalisation in 1948, the Great Western, along with its patrons and partisans, had more to lose than any of the other three. For over a century its prestige had been steadily building up to become almost a paragon in the estimation of its adherents. This was based on a belief in its own distinctiveness and its superiority in operation, its sound policies, and its historic achievements. It possessed a certain aloofness, and this was much in evidence in the further belief that its locomotives were second to none.

Perhaps it all began with Isambard Kingdom Brunel, who was its first constructional engineer. His dynamic career contributed so much to the romance of the railway and other prodigious development, until his early death in 1859. His broad gauge of 7 ft 0¼ in. between the rails was one of the results of his individualism. Despite the comparatively early demise of both the broad gauge and his steamship 'Great Eastern', nothing seemed to detract from Brunel's outstanding genius. Contemporary with Brunel was Sir Daniel Gooch, who from 1837 to 1864 as Locomotive Superintendent, was building the seven-footers Brunel so strongly advocated. Gooch came back from cable-laying with the *Great Eastern* in 1845 to become Chairman of the G.W.R., and later it fell to him to change over to standard gauge.

It is, of course, necessary to go back in time to state briefly how Great Western

Right: The principal workshops for the construction and repair of Great Western locomotives was at Swindon, in Wiltshire. Here in the erecting shop, large prairie tank No. 6106 is under heavy repair, flanked by locomotives of BR standard and LMSR origin, on 21 June 1964. 6106 is now preserved at Didcot. (*Derek Tuck*)

Right: A scene typical of many Great Western locomotive sheds (usually referred to as Running and Maintenance depots). At Radyr, north of Cardiff, 2–6–2 tanks Nos. 4177 and 4160, 2–8–2 tank No. 7242 and 0–6–0 pannier tank No. 3408 await their next turn of duty, on 19 July 1959. (*John Tarrant*)

NORTH STAR

FLYING DUTCHMAN
3009

Above: 260 of the legendary Dean Good's '2301' 0–6–0s were built; operation spanned the years 1883–1957. Here No. 2329 heads a freight away from Bridgnorth to Shrewsbury in 1937. (*I. Button*)

Top left: One of the Great Western Railway's earliest locomotives was the 2–2–2 *North Star*, built in 1837, by R. Stephenson & Co. It operated on Brunel's broad gauge, 7 ft 0½ in. (*British Rail*)

Bottom left: The appearance of Great Western locomotives was second to none; the Dean 4–2–2s of the 1890s are often considered to be the most graceful ever to run. Here is No. 3009 *Flying Dutchman*. (*British Rail*)

Right: Less popular were Dean's 'Aberdare' double-framed 2–6–0s, eighty-one being built between 1899 and 1902. All were withdrawn by 1949, including 2648, seen at Plymouth Laira on 12 April 1936. It lasted until 1944. (*W. A. Camwell*)

locomotives evolved, because so many of those in service in the 1930s, 40s and 50s were designed long before that date. Under Gooch, Joseph Armstrong became Locomotive Superintendent until 1886. He and his brother, followed by others, played a very significant part for many years, but the line of engine builders and designers for the G.W.R. is remarkable for its continuity. From 1864 to 1947 there were only five, and all but the last gave twenty years or more and all were steeped in G.W.R. traditions throughout their careers. This continuity is seen in the appearance of the various classes of locomotives they produced, for although development was always towards larger, taller engines as on other lines, especially for passenger services, they all possessed the same unmistakable outline.

Although some conversion to standard gauge for both locomotives and track was effected by Joseph Armstrong, it was a long and painful process. Dean took over in 1877, but it was not until 1892 that the last of the broad-gauge track had gone. No broad-gauge engines were built after 1866, but for many years there was a shortage of power because of the change-over. The oldest of the seven-footers were scrapped, but many had to be converted to 4 ft $8\frac{1}{2}$ in. rather than scrap and then build new, because this was much less expensive. Another of Dean's problems was to build standard gauge which could readily be converted temporarily to use on the broad gauge still in existence. This involved using double frames to make them fully convertible, as well as arranging accessories such as springs to fill changing needs. At the time, the Great Western had too little capacity for building new in spite of having works at both Wolverhampton and Swindon.

During Dean's reign, 1877 to 1902, 727 new engines were built at Swindon, of which 270 were tanks. Many of his were still in service when the 1923 Grouping took place, but though the era of the large single driving wheel went out with the old century, his 0–6–0 'Dean Goods' were still commonplace, as were several tanks. This period was one in which the placing of steam domes and main engine frames was unresolved. Some designs had large, brass-covered domes on the boiler, others were domeless. Some engines had the more conventional inside frames, which hid

Above: 'City' 4–4–0 *City of Truro* at Swindon shed on 4 September 1960. Credited with achieving 102 mph down Wellington bank, Somerset, in 1904, this locomotive exhibits the transition from Dean to Churchward practice. It operated special trains from 1957 until 1961, and is now in the Great Western Railway Museum at Swindon. (*John Tarrant*)

Top right: Churchward's 2-cylinder 'Saint' Class were a success after conversion from 4–4–2s to 4–6–0s. No. 2920 *Saint David* was the last survivor of seventy-seven engines

when withdrawn in 1953. (*D. J. Montgomery Collection*)
Centre right: The only Pacific built by the Great Western Railway was No. 111 *The Great Bear*. Its reputation was poor, and not enhanced by its very restricted route availability. It was rebuilt as a 4–6–0 in 1924, and is seen at Old Oak Common, London. (*Real Photos Ltd.*)
Bottom right: Churchward achieved further success with the 4-cylinder 'Star' Class of 1906. No. 4061 *Glastonbury Abbey* is seen on a Stephenson Locomotive Society special at Swindon Works on 11 September 1955. (*Brian Moone*)

the springs; others had the frames outside, or 'sandwich' double frames, with springs well clear above each wheel and, where coupled driving wheels were used, with the coupling rod working clear of the frame and splashers. Practically all had inside cylinders, including what are regarded as Dean's masterpieces, the '3001' Class single driver 4–2–2 for express passenger, and the '2301' 0–6–0, the 'Dean Goods'.

Dean's failing health from 1895 allowed his chief assistant, G. J. Churchward, to gradually bring in his own ideas. By the time he took over entirely in 1902, the design of Great Western locomotives had taken a different direction. It was a period of experiment motivated by the need for more power to give faster running on expresses, and to enhance the G.W.R. reputation for distinctively pleasing design which Dean had built up. Churchward was a great believer in standardisation, and if the period was one in which a good many changes were evolved, it had the ultimate aim of arriving at standard types which could serve every need of the G.W.R. for the foreseeable future. Swindon, enlarged and modernised, was becoming the power house, with boilers and other parts even being prefabricated to serve these needs, as experimental designs reached fruition. Although some standardisation had been carried out by Dean, to Churchward it was of vital concern. He reduced the types of boilers firstly to four sizes, driving wheels to three and cylinder sizes to two. His next step came with the building of a prototype for each type, designed for a specific purpose so as to test out its capabilities. He then made any modifications found to be necessary before embarking on a building programme in quantity. This process was naturally time-consuming, and building of older types had to continue. These included the double-framed 'Bulldogs', 'Atbaras' and 'Aberdares', and the double-framed tanks, but the new standard boilers were used. The 4–4–0 'Atbaras', some of which were given the names of flowers, were built by Churchward in 1903 and quickly achieved fame on expresses. Others were given 'City' names and in 1904 *City of Truro* was credited with a speed of 102 m.p.h.; these locomotives could perform non-stop runs between London and Plymouth.

The Belpaire firebox design, embodying a wide flat top to the firebox, was much favoured. The handsome brass safety valve cover, and copper-capped chimney,

Below: One of Churchward's best designs was the heavy freight 2–8–0, built between 1903 and 1919. The design of these 2-cylinder locomotives was modified by C. B. Collett, and further examples were built between 1938 and 1942, until a total of 167 were at work on the Great Western Railway on heavy freight duty, notably on the routes from South Wales to London and the Midlands. The engines were only finally ousted by dieselisation in the sixties. No. 3808, a 1939 Collett engine with screw reverse and side window cab, heads out of Birmingham for South Wales. Photographed between Small Heath and Tyseley, on 23 January 1965. (*Derek Smith*)

Above: The history of the 'large prairie' 2–6–2 tanks is extremely complicated. The Churchward design dates from 1903, though improvements were made under Collett in the 1930s, when large numbers were built for stopping passenger duties, trip freight work and banking. No. 5173, built at Swindon in 1931, is seen about to leave Cheltenham Spa St James's with a train for Kingham via Bourton-on-the-Water on 28 March 1959. Another locomotive of the same type is visible on the right. (*John Tarrant*)

whether or not a brass-covered dome was fitted, were features which set the stamp for the elegant Churchward design that remained a basic pattern for the remaining fifty years of the Great Western. A 4–6–0 passenger engine had appeared in 1902, which in some respects was rather American in appearance, but the next year an improved version emerged, still as a prototype, along with prototypes of a 2–8–0 heavy freight design, and a 2–6–2 mixed traffic tank type.

In his determination to seek the best, Churchward did not rely solely on past G.W.R. practice for future development. His 4–6–0 had in fact been influenced by American practice, and having heard of the de Glehn Compounds' success in France, placed an order for an Atlantic-type 4–4–2 to use under tests against his

Right: Between 1931 and 1935 seventy 'large prairies' were built with boilers pressed to 225 lbf/in.² instead of 200 lbf/in.², principally for London suburban duties. No. 6112 was recorded at Reading Great Western shed on 27 September 1958. (*John Tarrant*)

4566

5545
5545

Left: The 175 'small prairie' tanks were the mainstay of branch lines; No. 4566 of 1924 heads the 16.30 Bridgnorth to Bewdley train along the Severn Valley line between Eardington and Hampton Loade on 5 April 1976. (*Steve Owen*)
Below: Later engines had slightly increased water capacity. No. 5545 of 1928 was outside Penzance depot on 22 August 1962. (*Michael Hale*)
Right: Five outside cylindered dock shunters were built in 1910, numbered 1361–5. 0–6–0 saddle tank No. 1363 is shown at Plymouth Laira in the summer of 1960. 1363 is now preserved at Didcot. (*Allan Preston*)

own prototypes. This was four-cylindered; compounded by having steam pass through one cylinder and into a second before being exhausted through the chimney. For reasons of his own, Churchward progressed with a 4–4–0 class named after Counties, even though the 'Cities' were doing excellent work. The 'Counties' were not a success, and the 'Cities' survived them, along with the tank version which both types included.

Churchward's efforts to standardise were exhaustive, and many experimental designs were produced in order to find the best. He left nothing to chance, and even imported more de Glehn four-cylinder compound Atlantics from France for further tests. But he found that compounding was no real advantage, and nor was he satisfied that the de Glehn outside Walschaerts valve gear was superior to having cylinders outside with the Stephenson's valve motion inside. The fact that the latter method was in keeping with Great Western tradition was enough to tip the scales, and so it remained for years to come. Decisions were therefore made only when every alternative had been carefully studied, with designs emerging step by step until finality was reached.

The 'Saint' Class of 1903 was the basic design to be used for fast passenger work. Although it began as a 4–4–2 and seventy-seven were built, it had the ingredients for greater adhesion and power modified as a 4–6–0. This even inspired Churchward to go one better in 1908 and build a Pacific, the first ever to appear in Britain. Named

Previous page lower: The Churchward 2–8–0 tanks, built between 1910 and 1940, were important members of the standardised 'family' of Great Western engines, and the 205 engines served almost exclusively in South Wales. No. 4227 of 1913 was photographed at Newport Ebbw Jcn shed on 21 February 1960, and at that time possessed inside steam pipes and square running plate arrangement. It was modernised a few months later. (*D. C. Williams*)

Left: The later modifications to the 2–8–0 tanks are demonstrated in this view of No. 5226 of 1924 passing the site of Fountainbridge Halt between Caerphilly and Machen with a coal train on 4 August 1964. This locomotive was tested on the Lickey Incline in 1960. (*Michael Hale*)

Left: The nine Churchward 47XX 2–8–0s, built between 1919 and 1923, were elusive machines, for they frequently worked fast freight trains at night between London and Birkenhead, and London and Bristol, only gaining passenger duties to the West Country in the summer period. No. 4707 is seen at Reading shed on 26 April 1959. (*Michael Hale*)

Left: Churchward mixed traffic 2–6–0 No. 6368 photographed whilst double-heading 0–6–0 No. 2246 on the Locomotive Club of Great Britain, 'Thames, Avon and Severn', railtour at Stratford-upon-Avon on 12 October 1963. (*Derek Tuck*)

Above: 342 of the ubiquitous Churchward moguls were built during the period 1911–32 for mixed traffic duties. No. 4358, newly shopped at Caerphilly Works, is shown at Swindon shed on 16 June 1957, awaiting its next duty. At the time, No. 4358 (built in 1914) was the oldest of the type in service. (*Michael Hale*)

The Great Bear, it proved to be too heavy for many tracks and bridges, and it was not long before it had to be confined to a few routes, leaving Churchward to concentrate on 4–6–0s, but with an enhanced reputation for himself and the G.W.R. from the publicity received. The 'Saints' weighed 72 tons, engine only, and having tried *North Star* in 1906 as a 4–4–2 Atlantic, he brought out *Dog Star* in 1907 as a 4–6–0 weighing $75\frac{1}{2}$ tons.

The 'Stars' as well as the 'Saints' had a working pressure of 225 lb/in.^{2}. This was considerably higher than for other companies, but Churchward had seen proof of the need for high pressure from tests with the de Glehn, which ran at 227 lb. Another important feature which became standard was the tapered boiler. This

Right: The 2 ft $6\frac{1}{2}$ in. gauge Welshpool and Llanfair Railway was part of the Cambrian, and later part of the Great Western Railway. Its two locomotives built in 1902 were Nos. 822 *The Earl* and 823 *Countess*. After closure in 1956, the line was rescued for preservation and the two locomotives returned to the line from Oswestry Works. Here, *Countess* busies herself at Llanfair Caerinion in the summer of 1966. (*Dave Cooke*)

Left: In 1923 the Great Western absorbed some independent South Wales Companies, of which the Taff Vale and Rhymney were the most important. Many of the locomotives were rebuilt with Great Western boilers, and Taff Vale 'A' class 0–6–2 tank No. 397 is a typical example, seen here at Quakers Yard Low Level on 26 June 1956. It was built in 1920 and scrapped in 1957. (*Brian Moone*)

reduced tube deterioration just as the Belpaire firebox, to which it was attached, increased the heating surface. The dome was discarded and in some respects the general appearance of these early 'Stars' and 'Saints' was rather austere. Churchward had admired the purely functional American approach, and had to some extent practised it until it was realised that, in so doing, his engines lacked the grace and finish of those being evolved by rival C.M.E.s. He had followed the typically British practice of keeping outside pipework and fittings to a minimum for the sake of giving a sleek uncluttered appearance, and had dispensed with the steam dome. After 1907, he began to pay more attention to the finer points of appearance.

The introduction of superheating, also in 1906, was a rather important landmark in Churchward's career. This too was the subject of experiment, the first tried being the Schmidt fire tube. The general principle of superheating is to make steam pass from the boiler through tubes exposed to intense heat, so as to dry it out and make it even more powerful. It was an addition, as a final stage, to the vital heating surface factor. The Swindon No. 3 superheater was the outcome of tests between 1906 and 1909, and it remained standard until the end.

4–6–0s were built to both two- and four-cylinder designs in the belief that two were sufficient on easy routes, whilst four were best for long and more severe hauls. The latter were 'simple'; compounding had been discontinued. After a time it was found that the fours were smoother running because of better balance and less torque or thrust as well as having the edge on hauling capacity; they frequently

Top right: Just as the 0–6–2 tank was the usual South Wales main line locomotive, so the 0–6–0 tank was the choice for shunting and trip work. Port Talbot Railway saddle tank No. 813, built in 1901, operated from Duffryn Yard depot until purchased by Backworth Colliery in 1934. This view shows the locomotive at Bewdley, Severn Valley Railway, in September 1976. (*D. C. Williams*)

Right: The Swansea Harbour Trust operated a unique collection of Peckett 0–4–0 saddle tanks which were also taken over by the Great Western Railway. After the closure of Danygraig shed, some of these locomotives were sent to Swansea East Dock depot, where 1151 was the last survivor early in 1962. It was built in 1913. (*Allan Preston*)

Bottom left: A scene on the 1 ft 11½ in. gauge Vale of Rheidol Railway at Devil's Bridge. No. 7 *Owain Glyndwr* is one of three 2–6–2 tanks that still operate the line, and are based at Aberystwyth. No. 7 was built in 1923 and is now one of the last three steam locomotives owned and operated by BR. (*Jarrolds*)

GREAT WESTERN
813

Left: Collett's 'Castles' were the mainstay of express passenger services from 1923 until dieselisation in the sixties. No. 5090 *Cleeve Abbey*, rebuilt from 'Star' No. 4070 which carried the same name, is seen on the disposal road at Wolverhampton Stafford Road depot on 5 March 1961. No. 5090 ran as an oil burner for a short time in 1947. (*Michael Hale*)

Below: No. 7023 *Penrice Castle*, actually built under BR auspices in 1949, speeds over Goring water troughs, between Reading and Didcot, with a Paddington to Worcester and Hereford express on 29 September 1962. (*Derek Smith*)

Right: No. 5054 *Earl of Ducie* is about to leave Oxford with the down 'Cathedrals Express' from Paddington to Worcester and Hereford on 10 June 1964. No. 5054 is paired with a flush-sided Hawksworth tender; it was withdrawn a short time later still in fine mechanical trim, having achieved 100 mph on a test run down Honeybourne bank. (*Derek Tuck*)

Bottom right: The fine finish of Great Western engines is shown in this view of the nameplate of 'Castle' No. 5017. This Gloucester-based engine was thus renamed in 1954 to commemorate the achievements of the 'glorious Gloucesters'. (*Max Lock*)

worked twelve and fourteen coaches at 60 m.p.h. The twos, however, had the better acceleration, but this had to be restricted because anything near full throttle created such a sharp exhaust blast that it caused the fire to lift and to emit live sparks through the chimney. To obviate this, a specially designed baffle had to be fitted on the top of the blast pipe, known as the 'jumper top'. This also made for smoother acceleration, with a lessening of rhythmic pull which passengers in the front coaches could feel with each piston thrust of the engine.

Seventy of the 'Star' Class were built in the period up to 1913. This period was one of great progress for the G.W.R. Its reputation soared, with some direct and important long-distance routes having named trains, such as the 'Cornish Riviera Express' to Penzance, the 'Cheltenham Flyer', and the 'Ocean Mail' to Plymouth and Fishguard, which were then ports of call for Atlantic liners. The 'Star' is reckoned to be the most successful of any British passenger design prior to 1923.

The 1914–18 war put an end to new designs, and the G.W.R. was placed under Government control along with the other companies. Much of Churchward's reputation was due to his new passenger locomotives, but he had not neglected the freight train needs, or those of short-route passenger trains for which tanks and the older 0–4–2s were used. It is worth noting that, whilst the freight train mileage covered in the 1900–8 period fell by fourteen per cent, the actual tonnage carried rose by thirty-five per cent. The 2–8–0s carried the heaviest coal traffic, with loads of sixty-five wagons on the more severe sections of track from South Wales and up to

Left: 200 Collett 0–6–2 tanks of the 56XX class were built by Swindon and outside contractors between 1924 and 1928; they were intended to replace ageing locomotives of non standard but similar design in South Wales. One of the exceptions was 1926-built No. 5658 of Tyseley, here seen bustling a van train along the North Warwickshire line approaching Hall Green on the evening of 5 June 1962. (*Michael Mensing*)

eighty between Swindon and London. The 'Aberdares' were also used for this important traffic, while the 2–6–2 tanks did good service on short freight routes. With standardisation in full swing, wheel diameter was the principle variable factor. The largest was, of course, for the express passenger services, the smallest for the heaviest freight, and in between were those for mixed traffic, and local or suburban passenger trains.

The Edwardian period was also the heyday of the steam-driven rail coach, mounted on two bogies. On one was fitted a vertical multi-tube boiler. The coupled wheels were powered by two small outside cylinders, and though the fireman had to remain on the confined footplate, the driver had controls at both ends. A total of ninety-nine of these little self-propelled cars were built to suit the limited service they performed. Speed, too, was limited, and they later gave way to two-coach trains headed by a small independent tank engine, mainly because of the maintenance problem of a locomotive and coach combined.

Many of the older designs were rebuilt rather than scrapped. Wherever possible new standard parts were used, but the old single wheelers were something of a problem in this respect. Eighty of the '3001' 4–2–2 Class were still in use in 1907, and the standard tapered boiler would not go between the huge driving wheels. Some were fitted with parallel boilers, but the oldest were withdrawn. The last survived until 1915, the same year in which the smaller 2–2–2 single-wheeler likewise ended its long career.

Top right: 'The Kings' were the pride of the Great Western fleet, thirty being built from 1927 to 1930. No. 6013 *King Henry VIII* approaches Bentley Heath near Solihull with the 06.45 Wolverhampton to Paddington express on 30 June 1961. (*Michael Mensing*)

Bottom left: No. 2900 *Saint Martin* was rebuilt in 1928 and became the prototype of the 'Hall' Class, taking the number 4900. Its lower pitched boiler is apparent in this view taken at Swindon Works on 7 September 1958, when the locomotive was used on a Stephenson Locomotive Society special from Birmingham Snow Hill. No. 4900 was withdrawn in 1959. (*Max Lock*)

Right: No. 6003 *King George IV* is ready to back down from Old Oak Common depot to Paddington Station to take on an express on 25 October 1959. All the 'Kings' were withdrawn after dieselisation of London to Birmingham services in 1962. (*John Tarrant*)

6013
A05

With seven sizes of boiler now standardised at Swindon, rebuilding of old but not outworn designs was no great problem. They could be used on engines needed for both passenger and goods services, and for both tender and tank engines. In tanks, Churchward began quite a family of 2–6–2s with the introduction of his '3100' Class, for it later developed into four power grades. Three were very sturdy, weighing just about 80 tons, and having boiler pressure of 200 to 225 lb/in.^{2}. A lighter variety weighed 61 tons, and possessed 175 lb/in.^{2} boiler pressure. Although only five of the '3100' Class were built, over the years the other three types between them exceeded 400 examples. All had the now-standard outside cylinders with inside valve gear.

The family of small tanks was not so similar in appearance. These were mostly 0–6–0s for shunting and short hauls, but the squat little 0–4–2 was used extensively for suburban traffic. This, and some other classes, had straightforward side tanks varying in length according to the required water capacity. But there were also saddle tanks, the fitting of which involved a hole on top through which the steam dome protruded. A third type, common only on the G.W.R., was the pannier tank – an 0–6–0 engine, with tanks fixed to both sides of the boiler and not directly attached to the frame. Many of these were used in the South Wales coalfields, and were quite common until the last days of steam, some eventually being purchased by the National Coal Board for its own use.

With the introduction of 2–6–0 mixed traffic tender engine No. 4301 in 1911, Churchward had virtually met every requirement of motive power for the whole of the G.W.R. system. So it was that between 1911 and 1922 no major new designs were introduced. There were, of course, variations on those existing, but the 'Saints' and 'Stars' continued to be built, along with tank versions of many standard types, including the 2–8–0s, and 0–6–0s purely for freight. Wartime building of the latter was especially strong, and many of the 2–6–0s as well as 2–8–0s were shipped overseas as part of the war effort. South Wales coal alone called for great effort, for the huge British Navy had to be supplied. All ships were coal-fired, and a battleship at sea consumed up to 350 tons of Welsh coal per day. Churchward's fruitful reign as C.M.E. ended with his retirement in 1921. He was killed on the line outside Swindon Works twelve years later, but one can be certain that he had kept in close touch with his successor, C. B. Collett. With the benefit of experience under Churchward, what was to be one of the most successful of all G.W.R. express engines – the 'Castle' Class – was probably being developed when Collett took over. It was introduced in 1923, the year in which the 'Grouping' took place.

Of the four systems – the other three being the London & North Eastern, Southern, and London, Midland & Scottish – the Great Western was the least affected by this wholesale amalgamation. It not only retained its name unaltered, but benefited by the absorption of smaller companies. These were principally the Cambrian, covering Central Wales, and the Taff Vale and Rhymney companies in South Wales. They added no great distance to the 2,700 miles already owned but

Below left: The most prolific steam locomotives in Britain were the Great Western 57XX 0–6–0 pannier tanks, 863 examples being built between 1929 and 1949. They were to be seen all over the Great Western system and after nationalisation in other areas also. They were equally effective on shunting duties or 50 mph passenger trains. No. 5764, built in 1929, was sold to London Transport for engineer's train duty in 1960 and resold to the Severn Valley Railway in 1970. Here it sets out across Bewdley North Viaduct for Arley on 4 December 1976. (*D. C. Williams*)

Right: No. 8701 photographed at Coleford (Severn and Wye) during a Stephenson Locomotive Society tour of the Forest of Dean lines on 13 May 1961. Sandwiched between two pairs of auto coaches is large-wheeled pannier No. 6437. (*John Warr*)

Below: More typical of the latter-day condition of panniers is Worcester's No. 3682, photographed at the home depot in 1963. No. 3682 was built at Swindon in 1940 and scrapped in 1965. Later engines were built with the higher cab. (*John Tarrant*)

filled up gaps in what could be termed G.W.R. territory. The Railway was thus in a much stronger position to forge ahead than any of the other three, for apart from having increased its scope, it had already standardised to a large extent with locomotives of proven worth. Above all, perhaps, there was no break in its executive control. Including engines taken over from the smaller companies in the amalgamation, the G.W.R. now had 1,486 tender engines, 2,415 tanks and 63 rail cars.

The 'Castle' Class was largely based on the 4–6–0 'Star', the only one of Churchward's final designs with four cylinders. 'Castles' were given larger boilers and cylinders and, of the 161 built, fifteen were in fact rebuilds from 'Stars'. And one other was *The Great Bear*, rebuilt as a 4–6–0 with a new boiler. Working pressure remained at 225 lb/in.^{2}, and the weight of the engine only was slightly under 80 tons. From the first, 'Castles' created a stir. Whilst the other companies, except perhaps the L.N.E.R., were floundering, the G.W.R. was a little smug about its achievement, especially when a 'Castle' lent to the L.M.S. in 1925 proved superior to anything that company possessed. Interchange trials with the first L.N.E.R. Pacifics proved a similar result. The net result of this was the spread of Great Western ideas in locomotive design in some degree to the other three systems. It led indirectly to the L.M.S. bringing out the 4–6–0 *Royal Scot*. To cap it all, the

Above: Mixed traffic 4–6–0 No. 5951 *Clyffe Hall* (1924–65) shunts in Gloucester Central Station, fresh from overhaul at Swindon Works on 28 March 1959. 330 'Halls' were built between 1928 and 1950, including the 'Modified Hall' series, or 6959 class, introduced from 1944 onwards. The design was an updating of the highly successful 'Saint' Class of 1902. (*John Tarrant*)

Top right: No. 5992 *Horton Hall* bursts out from the girders above Birmingham Snow Hill's platform 12 with a passenger train for the West Country in the summer of 1963.
(*Allan Preston*)

Bottom right: No. 5978 *Bodinnick Hall* heads an eastbound freight on the slow line near Cholsey and Moulsford, east of Didcot, on 29 September 1962. 5978 and 5992 survived until dieselisation in 1965.
(*Derek Smith*)

Left: 2251 'Collett Goods' 0–6–0 No. 3218 leaves Wells Priory Road, with the 10.35 Yatton local on 6 September 1963. The design dates from 1930, and 3218 was built at Swindon in 1948. (*David Idle*)
Right: The 14XX Class (48XX until 1946) 0–4–2 tanks were used on light branch lines; seventy-five were built from 1932–6, and also twenty non-push-and-pull locomotives. No. 1420 was photographed at Leominster on 25 March 1962. It now operates on the Dart Valley Railway in Devon. (*John Tarrant*)
Bottom right: No. 1453 leaves St Mary's Crossing Halt with a Gloucester–Chalford local in September 1964. Speeds of 70 mph were achieved on these trains. (*Allan Preston*)
Bottom: 'Collett Goods' No. 3201 at Oswestry shed in 1957, coupled to a tender off a withdrawn ROD 2–8–0. The forty-three ton locomotive was coupled to a forty-seven ton tender! (*Max Lock*)

appointment of William Stanier, with his G.W.R. training, as C.M.E. to the L.M.S. led to even more Great Westernry in his designs for that company.

The 'Castles' established Collett's reputation, and the G.W.R. Publicity Department took every advantage offered by their performance to enhance prestige and attract customers, and several more through-train routes were launched. In point of fact, Collett was more outgoing than was Churchward, who tended to keep his intentions as well as his practices well guarded. Collett was in much friendlier rivalry with other C.M.E.s – Fowler, Gresley and Maunsell – and they frequently met for discussions and exchanges of views. He had several engines in different

1420

classes built by outside firms, including a little 0–4–0 with outside cylinders and Walschaerts valve gear built by Avonside of Bristol. The new 0–6–2 tanks, of which 200 were built, were also a departure from G.W.R. practice. They were substitutes for some of the older Welsh engines which, having been absorbed, were gradually replaced in the interests of standardisation.

The demands of the Traffic Department for power equal to the task of pulling heavier coaching stock to faster timings led to Collett bringing out the 'Kings' in 1927. It was his first real break with the stricter Churchward tradition, although in general appearance it was an enlarged version of a 'Castle'. The tapered boiler was longer and wider, as were the cylinders, and the pressure was stepped up to 250 lb/in.^{2}. Nominal tractive effort increased from 31,625 lb of the 'Castles' to over 40,000 in the 'Kings' and the weight of engine increased to 89 tons as compared with 79.

For such a locomotive – handsome and powerful but with no frills – the class name 'King' was quickly transferred from a late batch of 'Stars' as being more appropriate. To No. 6000, the first of the batch, was given the name of the reigning monarch, King George V – no doubt with publicity in mind. And it took to the rails a few weeks before Fowler brought out his *Royal Scot* for the L.M.S., so maintaining the G.W.R. lead. For further publicity, No. 6000 was shipped to America in the autumn of 1927 for the Centenary of the Baltimore and Ohio Railroad, and ran a series of exhibition trips on other railroads before returning to Cardiff Docks. After fifty years, No. 6000 still comes to life in preservation.

The 'Hall', 'Grange' and 'Manor' Class locomotives successively introduced by Collett in 1928, 1936 and 1938 were all 4–6–0s. They followed the by then familiar G.W.R. outline; the 'Halls' and 'Granges' varying mainly in wheel size and firebox proportions. The 'Granges' had 5 ft 8½ in. wheels, and were classed as mixed traffic locomotives, whilst the 'Halls' at 6 ft 8½ in. were for fast passenger work, and a total of 330 were built, including several after 1948 when the G.W.R. was merely the Western Region of British Railways. Eighty 'Granges' were built, and only thirty 'Manors'. These were specially designed, with 5 ft 8½ in. wheels and a smaller but lighter boiler, to meet the restrictions of some lines on weight, especially the former

Above: Collett 0–6–0 pannier tank No. 6412, built in 1934, takes refreshment at Stroud whilst working an auto train from Gloucester to Chalford in autumn 1964. This locomotive was withdrawn shortly afterwards and is now to be seen on the West Somerset Railway at Minehead. Forty locomotives of the type were built between 1932 and 1937. (*John Warr*)

Right: Collett pannier tank No. 6435 was withdrawn in 1964, and restored at Worcester Works after private purchase. It is here seen on 24 April 1965 at Stratford-upon-Avon waiting for a Stephenson Locomotive Society special to return from a last trip over the Stratford and Midland Jcn. line. No. 6435 is now on the Dart Valley Railway. (*John Tarrant*)

Right: Six 0–6–0 tanks with outside cylinders were built in 1934, generally to the same design as the 1361 class but with pannier instead of saddle tanks. These 1366 Class engines were used on Weymouth Quay, Bridgwater docks and other restricted locations. Only when LSWR 2–4–0 well-tanks were withdrawn early in 1962 were several locomotives allocated to Wadebridge shed in Cornwall for working the mineral line to Wenford Bridge. Here No. 1369, now on the Dart Valley Railway, blasts uphill near Dunmere Jcn with china clay, on 24 August 1962. (*Michael Hale*)

Right: Between 1934 and 1938, fifty-four 2–8–0 tanks were rebuilt with extended bunkers and a rear pony truck. These 72XX locomotives were also used in South Wales, but several examples were based elsewhere. In this view, No. 7218 of Banbury shed heads light northwards for Banbury Yard to take over an iron ore train on 11 July 1964. (*Derek Tuck*)

Above: A Cambrian scene of the 1950s is here evoked on the Bluebell Railway on 26 February 1977. 'Dukedog' 4–4–0 No. 9017 was specially posed just outside Sheffield Park Station with a typical short freight train. The 'Dukedogs' consisted of an amalgam of the boiler of a 'Duke' Class with the chassis of a 'Bulldog' Class. No. 9017 was originally numbered 3217 and named *Earl of Berkeley* before the plates were transferred to a 'Castle'. No. 9017 operated from Machynlleth depot before withdrawal in 1960.
(*Peter Zabek*)

Cambrian Railways main line in Central Wales.

An outstanding feature of G.W.R. locomotive-building was the way in which successive C.M.E.s drew on older basic designs for new engines with a few modifications. The same applied to rebuilds. What had been a successful old design could serve modern needs by using new standard practices and fittings, which were themselves modern in their day. It applied to practically the whole range and even when the end of steam was near in 1948, the process continued. The various tanks, especially the panniers – which outnumbered any other type, whether tank or tender, were still being built in 1950.

Collett retired in 1941, and was followed as C.M.E. by F. W. Hawksworth – another man steeped in G.W.R. tradition. He had been with the company long enough to have made the drawings for *The Great Bear* in 1908. After 1944, he set out to improve G.W.R. practice still further. He concentrated on boiler design and brought out the 'Modified Hall' Class, embodying mainly boiler improvements, including an increased degree of superheating. Spurred on by the continuing need for improved mixed traffic locomotives, he brought out the 'County' Class 4–6–0 in 1945. These locomotives had two cylinders driving coupled wheels of 6 ft 3 in. diameter. The boiler was pressed to 280 lb/in.² for the first time in G.W.R. design. The locomotives were only moderately successful, not surprisingly in view of their

Bottom left: Eighty 'Grange' 4–6–0s were built between 1936 and 1939, for mixed traffic service. They were predominantly used for freight traffic, but were little inferior to the larger driving wheeled 'Halls' on passenger service, and were very popular amongst enginemen. No. 6848 *Toddington Grange* heads southwards through Oxford with freight in July 1964. No. 6848 was built at Swindon in 1937 and taken out of service in 1965. (*Derek Tuck*)

Right: 'Manor' 4–6–0 No. 7801 *Anthony Manor* is coupled ahead of 2–6–0 No. 7314 at Ruabon on 29 September 1962. The pair are ready to haul a Festiniog Railway Society special over the now closed line to Barmouth. Thirty of the 'Manor' 4–6–0s were built for operation over secondary lines where larger boilered engines would be too heavy. They were at their best on passenger duty in Central Wales and pilot work over the South Devon banks. *Anthony Manor* was built in 1938 and condemned in 1965. It spent many years at Chester West depot. (*John Tarrant*)

Right: 'Modified Hall' 6959 Class No. 7928 *Wolf Hall* is about to depart from Paddington with a Worcester express in 1963. No. 7928 was the penultimate engine of the class, built at Swindon in 1950 and withdrawn in 1965. The performance of the later engines was a little inferior to 'Castles' on the Worcester trains and maintenance was of a high order until almost the cessation of steam working. (*Allan Preston*)

employment on work normally ascribed to the larger 'Castle' 4–6–0s.

G.W.R. locomotive history was brought to a conclusion with three classes of 0–6–0 pannier tank; the mixed traffic '9400' which utilised a taper boiler within the '5700' layout; the '1500' Class, employing outside Walschaerts valve gear for the first time in G.W.R. practice and designed for heavy shunting; and the '1600' Class for ultra-light branch line work. The latter two designs only appeared after Nationalisation.

The principle ingredients for the success of the G.W.R. are not difficult to determine. Previous to the Grouping, a pattern had already become well established

Above: Shrewsbury 'County' No. 1017 *County of Hereford* has just arrived at its home town with a Plymouth to Manchester train on 4 July 1959. At Shrewsbury the 'County' will be removed in favour of an LM engine. The 'Counties' were not universally liked, though they steamed better when the original 280 lbf/in.^{2} boilers were reduced to 250 lbf/in.^{2}, and they did good work on the north-and-west route. (*John Tarrant*)

Left: The Stephenson Locomotive Society 'Farewell of the Counties' trip was run from Birmingham Snow Hill to Swindon on 20 September 1964. Here No. 1011 *County of Chester* approaches Oxford on the return journey. Thirty 'Counties' were built between 1945 and 1947, and withdrawal commenced in 1962. No. 1011 was the last survivor when the photograph was taken. (*Derek Tuck*)

Right: The Hawksworth 94XX panniers were introduced in 1947 as an updated version of the 57XX locomotives. Though equally effective on shunting they were more unstable than their predecessors on passenger work, and were not liked in this capacity. Ten were built in Great Western days, the remaining 200 in BR days by outside contractors. Nos. 3400–3409 were the last locomotives completed to a pre-nationalisation design. Here is 8481 of Radyr at Swindon on 24 March 1963. (*John Tarrant*)

Below: 94XX locomotives largely supplanted LMSR 'Jinties' on Lickey Incline banking duties in the late fifties. At this point the former LMSR Bristol–Birmingham line climbs the Lickey Hills at a gradient of one in thirty-seven for two miles. The freight train shown here requires the services of four 94XX panniers for its attack on the bank on 31 March 1962. (*John Tarrant*)

which included the vital factor of standardisation. It was reinforced by Churchward, whose vision and determination was to have a lasting effect until the very end of steam. It has resulted in a kind of cult for those who, for various reasons, regard the Great Western as the aristocrat of companies and its engines as supreme examples of the best in British locomotive design, practice and performance. The cult is as strong, if not stronger, now than when steam was king. It goes by the name of Great Westernry, and has many adherents.

Proof rests, they say, in the many G.W.R. features and practices taken up by other companies, and after 1948 in the B.R. standard designs. L.M.S. enthusiasts

claim that the B.R. Standard classes of the 1950s were largely based on Crewe designs, but they would be reminded that Stanier introduced them because he himself came from Swindon. Be that as it may, the G.W.R. was nothing if not realistic and 'led the way' in many respects. Not least of these was the precision machinery and testing as well as standardisation.

Representatives of many classes have been preserved, and some are in running condition. The Dart Valley Railway is almost entirely G.W.R. in its rolling stock, and a sprinkling of 'Kings', 'Castles' and 'Halls' remain here and there, including a 'Castle' in the Science Museum. Even pannier tanks have been rescued after lying derelict for years at the Barry scrapyard, but with so many variations on a large number of classes which the G.W.R. evolved, it is little wonder that some have vanished for ever. It may well be that steam nostalgia will remain for at least as long as relics remain and, for many, 'Great Westernry' will become an undying legend.

Left: Two classes of Hawksworth pannier tanks appeared in 1949. The 16XX class eventually consisted of seventy locomotives built by Swindon until 1955. They were to be found on branch lines throughout the system, with two examples in Scotland. Withdrawal commenced in 1959, with one example, No. 1659, lasting only five years. No. 1638 was one of a pair which survived into 1966 at Wrexham Croes Newydd depot. It was bought for preservation and now forms the backbone of Dart Valley Railway services from Buckfastleigh, where it was seen on 3 August 1977. (*D. C. Williams*)

Bottom left: No. 1502 was the third locomotive built at Swindon in 1949 of a class of ten locomotives designed for 'heavy shunting'. They were relatively unstable in this use, and were even more dangerous on empty stock workings around Paddington; their early replacement by diesel shunters was inevitable. Three were bought by the National Coal Board in 1961 and used at Coventry Colliery. No. 1501 was saved and is at Bewdley on the Severn Valley Railway. No. 1502 is shown at Coventry in August 1962 in the distinctive NCB livery.
(*John Tarrant*)

Top right: Pages 31 and 32 show a trio of 'Manor' 4–6–0s saved from the cutter's torch and running again to the delight of many who cannot recall the great days of steam. No. 7808 *Cookham Manor* and No. 6998 *Burton Agnes Hall* leave Ledbury tunnel on the return journey from Hereford to Didcot on 14 June 1975. The Great Western train and locomotives are all based at the Great Western Society's headquarters at Didcot and make main line outings several times each year.
(*Alan Wilkinson*)

Bottom right: No. 7827 *Lydham Manor* rounds Waterside curve between Goodrington and Churston, whilst working a Torbay and Dartmouth Railway train from Paignton to Kingswear on 15 September 1975.
(*D. C. Williams*)

7808

GREAT WESTERN

Above: No. 7819 *Hinton Manor* is seen leaving Northwood with a Severn Valley Railway train for Bewdley on 28 December 1977. No. 7819, built in 1939, was withdrawn from Shrewsbury in 1965 and languished at Barry Scrapyard in increasingly derelict condition until 1973. Renovation took several years and *Hinton Manor* began further service in 1977. (*Bob Green*)

Left: In the 1930s, a series of diesel railcars were built, the first successful attempt at operating these vehicles. Thirty-eight were built, the first eighteen of streamlined design, followed by twenty of 'razor edge' body design by Swindon. All had two AEC bus-type engines. The second batch were used for branch line work, like No. 22, shown at Hampton Loade in preservation. These cars last ran for BR in 1962. (*D. C. Williams*)

85306 837 2
© 1979 Jarrold Colour Publications
Printed by Jarrold & Sons Ltd, Norwich. 280PW

CHIEF MECHANICAL ENGINEERS

WILLIAM DEAN *(1877–1902)*
The work of this Victorian engineer was to be seen until the demise of Great Western steam in Britain, for the 57XX pannier tanks largely embodied the engineering of Dean's time. His locomotives were noted for their straightforward design and handsome appearance as evidenced by the graceful 4–2–2 singles. His 0–6–0 tender engines were famous even in Continental war service, and the range of 0–6–0 tank engines was an integral part of the Great Western scene.

GEORGE JACKSON CHURCHWARD *(1902–21)*
One of the greatest, if not the greatest of the twentieth-century locomotive engineers. He applied rational design and testing, first to locomotive boilers and then to cylinders and motion, before embarking on the introduction of a range of standard locomotive types for the Great Western Railway that was the envy of most British railways. The 'Stars' and 'Saints' were perhaps the best known, but 2–6–0s, 2–8–0s, 2–6–2 tanks and many others all came in for attention. Killed tragically during retirement by an express train passing Swindon Works.

CHARLES B. COLLETT *(1922–41)*
During this period of Great Western development, the great traditions of Churchward were continued. Collett was responsible for the introduction of the 'Castle' and 'King' 4–6–0s, designs which brought Great Western steam to its zenith. Continued building of established designs was punctuated by the introduction of new types employing many of the existing standard parts. Swindon products became known throughout the world in this period.

F. W. HAWKSWORTH *(1941–7)*
Hawksworth's tenure of office saw out Great Western steam design. Production of standard types continued despite wartime restrictions; Hawksworth is best remembered for his 'County' 4–6–0s and outside-cylindered pannier tanks. In this final phase, Great Western design was losing out slightly to competition, notably from the LMSR, but Hawksworth's administration took the Great Western through very difficult times and paved the way for Swindon to make more than a minor contribution to the standard locomotives of British Railways.

WHERE CAN GREAT WESTERN LOCOMOTIVES STILL BE FOUND?

Great Western Railway locomotives are well represented in railway preservation. First of all, British Railways only steam-worked line, the narrow gauge Vale of Rheidol Light Railway from Aberystwyth to Devil's Bridge must be mentioned. The Welshpool and Llanfair Light Railway is another narrow gauge line with locomotives formerly in Great Western Railway stock, as were briefly two locomotives now on the Tal-y-llyn Railway from Tywyn.

The Great Western Railway flavour comes across most strongly on two railways in Devon under the same management, the Torbay and Dartmouth, and the Dart Valley from Buckfastleigh. Strong representation of the Great Western Railway and its next-door neighbour the LMSR is to be found on the Severn Valley Railway from Bridgnorth to Bewdley. The West Somerset Railway based at Minehead is another former Great Western Railway line returned to operation.

The largest collection of Great Western Railway rolling stock assembled at a museum site is to be found at the Great Western Society's Didcot engine shed, near Reading. Equally important is the collection of five locomotives and smaller relics and displays at the Great Western Railway Museum at Swindon.

Great Western locomotives can be found in operation at Parkend (Forest of Dean), Quainton (near Aylesbury), the Worth Valley line in Yorkshire, the Bluebell Railway in Sussex, Birmingham Railway Museum at Tyseley and Bulmers Hereford Railway Centre; also NCB property at Maesteg, South Wales. Great Western locomotives will soon be running at Loughborough, Carnforth, the North Yorkshire Moors Railway, Oswestry and Telford.

In a short review it is impossible to cover the location of every preserved item of Great Western rolling stock, but the above should give a good general indication of where Great Western steam is still active.